Hydroponics

THE ESSENTIAL HYDROPONICS GUIDE: A STEP-BY-STEP HYDROPONIC GARDENING GUIDE TO GROW FRUIT, VEGETABLES, AND HERBS AT HOME

ANDY JACOBSON

ISBN: 153033604X
ISBN-13: 978-1530336043

Contents

The information herein is offered for informational purposes solely, and is universal as so. The presentation of the information is without contract or any type of guarantee assurance.

The trademarks that are used are without any consent, and the publication of the trademark is without permission or backing by the trademark owner. All trademarks and brands within this book are for clarifying purposes only and are the owned by the owners themselves, not affiliated with this document.

Foreword

"Plants do not grow merely to satisfy ambitions or to fulfill good intentions. They thrive because someone expended effort on them."

— **Liberty Hyde Bailey (1858 - 1954)**

Whilst expending my efforts on it for almost 30 years, I've been able to narrow down the science of hydroponics into a number of easy to follow and digestible steps. I even like to say that I've managed to transform this science into somewhat of an art form.

After a great deal of encouragement from my agricultural friends and family, I'm compelled to share with you the proven step-by-step methods for creating and managing your own successful hydroponic system. With this, you will have the tools needed to grow a selection of herbs, vegetables, and flowers at home - without the use of any soil.

It's undeniable that hydroponics allows for greater control over the challenging factors that soil brings. The ultimate goal of this book is to allow you to wave goodbye and say a final farewell to the stubbornness of soil.

I've been careful to address the necessary foundations for those just getting started in hydroponics. On top of this, more advanced techniques are outlined for those that wish to become a hydroponic hero!

This is the 'go to' concise reference guide for hydroponics that covers: An introduction to hydroponics, hydroponic mediums, hydroponic systems, plant nutrition, lighting, the growing process, how to build your own homemade systems, and much more! This is all presented with clear explanations, photos and diagrams.

For your best understanding and results, I recommend reading this book in the order it has been structured with. This will put you on the steady path to complete frugality and self-sufficiency!

Best Wishes,

Andy Jacobson

Section 1: What Is Hydroponics?

"If there is magic in this planet, it is contained in water."

— **Loren Eiseley (1907 - 1977)**

The explanation starts with water and its vital role in the life of plants. Water is the trusty vehicle that provides the transport of nutrients and energy (salts and sugars) to the cells within a plant. Hydroponics is simply the process of distributing water, preserving its quality, and providing it with the nutrients that allows plants to reach their full genetic potential. The series of automatic events that happen in an ideal natural setting results in the breakdown of organic nutrient salts that eventually end up in soil. Plants are then able to absorb these nutrient rich salts as a result of water in the soil from rainfall. The reality is that the soil and environments plants generally grow in are far from perfect. So the goal with hydroponics is to try to replicate what occurs in a perfectly natural setting. This is achieved by consistently enriching water with nutrients, and then making these available for absorption by our plants. We refer to this water that we provide as balanced 'nutrient solution'.

The nutrient solution that you will supply is generally provided through a man-made enclosed system. This gives rise to the benefit of avoiding the evaporation that occurs in soil. In other words, we're ensuring that this nutrient rich water is always available to our plants when they require it. Whether you know it or not, it's likely that you've already practiced simple hydroponics by putting flowers in a vase and adding a ready-made nutrient solution.

Looking at the process more literally, the term 'Hydroponics' derives from Greek which translates to 'Water Work'. When you create your first hydroponics system you'll be providing nutrient rich 'Water' that is made available to your plants by a force of gravity or a pump that 'Works' to make this available for the roots of your plants.

You might now be asking the question: So how did hydroponics start being used in the first place? Many faced challenges whilst growing crops in ancient times, and due to a range of difficulties with pestilence, large numbers of crop yields were devastated. The lack of crops had severe consequences for countless communities, and this lead to a great deal of famine, along with conflicts between groups of people who were fighting for scarce crops. So the search was on to discover new methods of growing crops that did not solely rely on soil. People started to become aware of the effectiveness of growing plants in water. Some of the earliest hieroglyphic records of growing plants in water date back to a few hundred years BC. Between 372 and 287 BC, a Greek philosopher, Theophrastus investigated the nutrition of plants. Following this, an unofficial form of hydroponics was brought to use in the gardens of the Aztecs, the Chinese, and the hanging gardens of Babylon. Beginning in the 17th century, there was an emergence of scientific investigation into the biological makeup of plants. It was realized that the minerals a plant requires to grow is provided to the plant via the water in soil. This is what produced the finding that water alone could be used as a method of effectively growing crops and plants.

The initial terminology for this type of growing was known as 'nutriculture', and this was spread to commercially produced crops between 1925 and 1935. However it was not until the 1930s that the term 'hydroponics' was coined by W. F. Gericke, a professor at the University of California. Following that, the greenhouse industry started to incorporate hydroponics to tackle problems that were brought on by pests and diseases in soil. In modern agriculture, hydroponics is now used across numerous countries in vast greenhouses spanning tens of thousands of acres.

Hydroponics is consistently growing in popularity in the modern world, from backyard ventures to hydroponic applications on space stations! In fact, hydroponics will play a key role in being able to provide nutrition as humans continue to explore the possibility of living on other planets. On a more basic level, hydroponics provides an affordable means of producing nutrition for low-income areas of the world. For example, people living under tough conditions in desert areas Peru are able to satisfy their nutritional needs by using hydroponics. There are even branches of the United Nations that are investing in hydroponic education and providing subsides in order to help people in destitute conditions grow their own fruit and vegetables. The popularity of growing hydroponically as a hobby has gained a fair deal of popularity over recent decades. This now means that a huge range of hydroponic equipment is readily available both offline and online, making hydroponics a very accessible hobby to engage in.

Now that we have established what the process is about and it's roots, let's explore some of the many benefits of hydroponic gardening:

Improved genetic health: Plants in a hydroponic system are not only provided with nutrition that has a near to perfect composition, but they're also safeguarded from many potential pests that they could otherwise come into contact with when growing in soil. This allows the plants to reach a greater level of genetic health. As the saying goes, 'you are what you eat'.

High-scale production: Although hydroponics can be used to create your own variety of plants at home, an often surprising fact is that the hydroponic process is responsible for providing food to millions. The science has now been improved to a level at which more fruit, vegetables and herbs can be produced, at a higher quality than ever before! Yields from growing hydroponically are at least 20% greater than with growing with soil. As you can imagine, over a year this can create vast increases in the crops you are able to produce.

Affordable: Hydroponics will allow you to say goodbye to the often-costly ordeals of obtaining prepared soils and plant protection products. On top of this, most of the standard gardening tools (e.g. trowels, shovels, forks) are not needed.

Less-time, more produce: The process of planting becomes a breeze because you will no longer have to spend time preparing soil between planting. On top of this, your plants will be able to mature faster, generating you an abundance of beautiful produce.

Better looking, better tasting, and better for you: The conditions that you will create will give your plants the energy to do what they do best - grow! This results in produce that is superior in terms of size, taste, and nutritional value.

You will soon have the knowledge and tools to reap all of these benefits, so I hope by now you are completely sold on the process!

Although a hydroponic system creates a nutritional environment that is superior to soil, we still need to devise a 'medium' that is able to closely replicate the structural support that soil provides to plants. Thankfully, this is straightforward to achieve and we'll be exploring the different 'hydroponic mediums' in the next section.

Section 2: Choosing a Hydroponic Medium

"There exists everywhere a medium in things, determined by equilibrium."

— **Dmitri Mendeleev (1834 - 1907)**

The 'hydroponic medium' that I introduced in the last section is firstly used when we start off with seeds, but the medium is also useful for the growing of new plants from root cuttings. An ideal medium needs to have some specific qualities in order to be perfectly suited to hydroponics. First and foremost, the medium needs to be able to carry an equalized amount of water and air. It's important to consider that oxygen also plays a crucial role in plant growth; it allows for respiration that gives the plant energy to absorb the water and nutrients required for optimal growth. This perfect balance of air and water is achieved by finding a medium that has the correct sized holes between each fragment, also known as 'interstitial' spaces. You will also need a medium that has particles which do not conflict with the nutrient solution being used, and do not leak elements into the water being used in your system. This can cause pH levels to deviate away from the optimal level for growing. Another consideration is that the medium should be sterile and free from pest/disease organisms. If you are not confident about the sterility of your medium you can eliminate this risk by heating the medium to 160 degrees Fahrenheit – this can be done using a stove oven.

It is also worth ensuring that the chosen medium is affordable and easy enough to get hold of, along with being reusable.

I suggest that you the following consider the following mediums that have proven to satisfy these criteria, and can be used in the hydroponic systems that I'll be showing you how to build later.

Coconut Fiber:

'Coco fiber' comes from the husk of coconuts; it's 100% organic and makes for an excellent medium for hydroponic growing. Not only does it have a perfect amount of water and air retention, but it also protects from fungus. This renewable medium is also known as coco coir, or commercially as 'Cocopeat, 'Ultrapeat', and 'Coco-tek'. It's generally obtained as a compressed block that is placed in water to expand into a useable consistency.

Perlite:

Perlite is a type of volcanic glass - a classic hydroponic medium that's known to hold oxygen extremely well. The only downfall is that it's very lightweight which can pose problems if your hydroponic system is subject to forceful winds.

LECA:

Lightweight Expanded Clay Aggregate (LECA) is an entirely natural medium made from expanded clay granules. Its neutral pH levels and high water retention abilities makes for an ideal rooting solution.

Rockwool:

Deriving from melted rock and then made into fibers, Rockwool has been widely used in larger scale hydroponics. Again, this has great water retention and is also very competent in defending against any contaminants that can get into your hydroponic system. Despite being an effective medium, a downside is that it doesn't have a particularly environmentally friendly manufacturing process - this is something you may wish to consider.

A Modern Innovation - Starter Sponges:

Luckily enough, you can now get your hands on pre-made dynamic and biodegradable organic compost molds. These make for an excellent medium with perfect air/water retention and root protection. Also known as 'Perfect Starts', they're available to buy in a range of sizes making them a convenient and effective medium solution. They are certainly one of the best all-rounder mediums to get you started on your hydroponic venture.

Now that we have a sound understanding of the mediums that can be used to support the growth of our plants, this is now a great time to start considering the different types of hydroponic systems that are possible.

Section 3: Types of Hydroponic Systems

"A truly stable system expects the unexpected, is prepared to be disrupted, waits to be transformed."

— **Tom Robbins**

The hydroponic system is the main force in creating the desired conditions for our plants. These conditions supply roots with an ideal amount of nutrients, water and oxygen, along with removing the possibility of the dehydration of plant roots. The systems are either 'active' or 'passive'. Active systems have a power-driven apparatus that circulate plant nutrients, and passive systems rely on the natural force of gravity to deliver nutrients to your plants. The obvious advantage of an active system is that when set up efficiently, it can be left unsupervised in a greenhouse and feed your crops for weeks at a time!

Later on, you'll be learning how to plan and construct your very own hydroponic systems. To give you a better idea of hydroponics works in practice, it's important to familiarize yourself with the workings of some popular systems that are used today.

The Nutrient Film Technique (NFT):

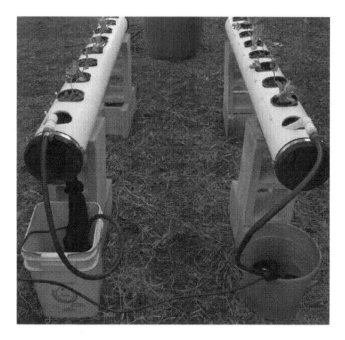

Within this system there is a tunnel in which plants are placed on top of with their roots exposed within the tunnel. The nutrient solution is placed in the tunnel and travels through it whilst making contact with the plant roots and then into a nutrient reservoir. Similar to the Dutch Bucket System, a pump recycles the nutrient solution directly back through the system. A distinct advantage of NFT is that the system is completely enclosed which creates a perfect level of humidity and removes the risk of root dehydration. This system is perfect for growing lettuce or any other short-term crops.

The Raft System:

This is known to be one of the most efficient and affordable systems available. Plants are supported on polystyrene sheets and float on a nutrient solution with their roots exposed. The solution is constantly being circulated and aerated to ensure oxygenation. Again, this is popular with lettuce and plants with rapid growth cycles.

The Dutch Bucket System:

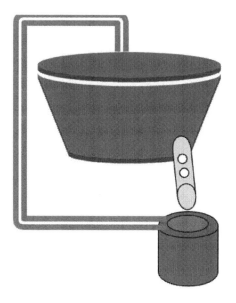

This method is often used by commercial growers and is effective when used with any of the growing mediums discussed previously. This system is best suited to longer-term crops such as tomatoes, peppers, basil, and even roses. The system is set up using a large bucket with a PVC pipe as a drain tube. The nutrient solution is placed into the bucket via a dripper which then drains through the drainpipe and into a reservoir as a result of gravity. A pump is then used to put the nutrient solution back into the bucket, and this cycle continues to repeat itself.

Autopot Self-Watering System:

An ideal system for those with little space and time. Once autopots are set up they run completely passively and are perfect for slow growing crops. This is a fairly modern development that has an automatic self-feeding system as a result of using a 'SmartValve' that feeds plants on demand - only when they need it - when the medium starts to dry. This closely replicates natural rainfall.

Aeroponics:

A more recent phenomenon is the aeroponic system in which roots are provided with nutrition and water mid-air. Plants are placed in baskets at the top of an enclosure. Their roots are exposed in the air inside the enclosure, and can then be sprayed with a nutrient solution. In terms of efficiency, this is a great system as roots only uptake the required amount of solution. The remainder is recycled and reused from the attached reservoir within the system. With such a system, it's crucial to maintain the surrounding humidity to sustain the hydration of the roots. This method has been proven to grow crops exponentially faster than when grown in soil.

A practical home-based application of aeroponics is vertical hydroponic gardening which is an excellent solution for those with limited space. We will be covering the steps on building your own system later on in the book.

Now that you have a general knowledge of how hydroponic systems operate, in the next section it's time to learn the details of the most important component that that stimulates the growth of your desired crops - plant nutrition.

Section 4: Plant Nutrition - Learning and Selecting

"Gardening involves so many disciplines: math, chemistry, reading, history."

— **David Chang**

Let's get started with some basic chemistry. Elements are what a plant uses for its living processes. Over 90% of a plant is made up of four key elements: Carbon, Hydrogen, Oxygen, and Nitrogen. As these elements make up the majority of a plant, it must be able to extract these elements in order grow efficiently. That said, a plant doesn't have to obtain these elements from a completely pure form. For example, although water (H20) is a compound (made up of more than one element), plants are able to extract the elements it needs as pure elements. As the four elements are crucial to a plants life, it's wise to be aware of some of their qualities.

Carbon:

This makes up over half of a plant's composition and is present in chlorophyll and the sugars that chlorophyll creates.

Hydrogen:

Plays a role in the process that results in roots absorbing nutrients. Hydrogen is extracted from water which also assists in maintaining a rigid structure in plants.

Oxygen:

Responsible for respiration which provides a plant energy to grow by creating sugars and starches.

Nitrogen:

Creates amino acids and chlorophyll that manufactures sugars.

Macro-nutrients

Although plants can extract the elements mentioned so far from a range of sources, it is 'Macro Nutrients' that generally make up plant solutions . These nutrients are what a plant extracts in bulk from the hydroponic medium that you use. These elements are Nitrogen (N), Phosphorus (P), and Potassium (K). You'll often see N-P-K levels on pre-made plant food packaging as an indication of strength. Macronutrients play crucial roles and should be regulated to be present in the correct quantities.

Too little Nitrogen results in weaker plants with small leaves, while an excess of Nitrogen poses crop-ripening issues. Phosphorus is responsible for fruit and flower creation, but too little results in poor root systems and weak flower generation. Potassium is the driver in protein synthesis which creates sugars and starch, and too little of it significantly slows plant growth.

Micronutrients

There are also other nutrients that plants extract in much smaller quantities. They are rarely in pre-made plant foods, but still have a range of considerable effects on a plant's living processes.

Calcium (Ca): Cell wall creation. Too little stunts growth.

Sulfur (S): Protein synthesis.

Iron (Fe): Chlorophyll development and sugar creation.

Magnesium (Mg): Chlorophyll and enzyme creation. Too little causes yellowing of leaves.

Boron (B): Combines with calcium for cell wall creation. Too little causes week stems.

Manganese (Mn): Creation of oxygen in photosynthesis. Too little causes yellowing of leaves.

Zinc (Zn): Respiration, chlorophyll, and nitrogen metabolism. A deficiency results in small leaves.

Copper (Cu): Enzyme activation; respiration and

photosynthesis. A deficiency results in pale and yellow leaves.

Selecting Your Hydroponic Nutrient

Beginner: pre-made nutrient solutions

As mentioned previously, you will likely see N-P-K percentages outlined on packaging for pre-made hydroponic nutrient solutions. N-P-K only makes up a part of the solution, with the rest comprising of filler and other nutrients that fuel the growth process. It's vital to remember that you can't use nutrient solutions that are designed for soil use. At first, it's best to search for a solution that is effective at growing a variety of crops. The correct concentration for the solution is crucial as the plants depend on what is mixed into the water that circulates around the system. That said, you'll easily find pre-made solutions with mixing instructions that correspond to your plants and the conditions that you're growing in. This makes things simple if you don't want the extra work of creating your own solutions. A warning - ensure that the packaging explicitly mentions that the nutrient solution is specifically designed for hydroponic practice.

Another factor to consider is whether the solution comes as a one-part solution that is better suited to a wider range of crops and growing conditions, or a two/three-part solution that is more customizable for specific types of crop and the stage in the growing process they are at. You will generally get better results with a two/three part solution, at the cost of being slightly more challenging to develop.

Advanced: mixing your own nutrient solutions

More advanced hydroponic growers often wish to mix their own solutions to suit the type of plants they're growing. In order to do this you will need to obtain the correct salts and dissolve them according to the following instructions. The following mixes create 1 gallon of nutrient solution, but these can be multiplied to suit your needs. For best results, it's important to try to get hold of high quality raw materials. As for the mixing process, fill a container with water warm enough to dissolve salt, and then proceed to dissolving each salt in the outlined quantities. It's best to add and dissolve each salt one at a time.

Nutrient Solution for Vegetable Crops (1 Gallon):

Calcium Nitrate ($Ca(NO_3)_2$): 6 grams

Potassium Nitrate (KNO_3): 2.09 grams

Sulfate of Potash (K_2SO_4): 0.46 grams

Monopotassium Phosphate (KH_2PO_4): 1.39 grams

Magnesium Sulfate ($MgSO_4$): 2.42 grams

7% Fe Chelated Trace Elements: 0.40 grams

Nutrient Solution for Fruit Crops (1 Gallon):

Calcium Nitrate (Ca(NO3)2): 8 grams

Potassium Nitrate (KNO3): 2.80 grams

Sulfate of Potash (K2SO4): 1.70 grams

Monopotassium Phosphate (KH2PO4): 1.39 grams

Magnesium Sulfate (MgSO4): 2.40 grams

7% Fe Chelated Trace Elements: 0.40 grams

Nutrient Solution for Flowering Crops (1 Gallon):

Calcium Nitrate (Ca(NO3)2): 4.10 grams

Potassium Nitrate (KNO3): 0.46 grams

Sulfate of Potash (K2SO4): 1.39 grams

Monopotassium Phosphate (KH2PO4): 1.39 grams

Magnesium Sulfate (MgSO4): 2.40 grams

7% Fe Chelated Trace Elements: 0.40 grams

n.b. The Chelated Trace Element needs to be made up of:

Iron - 7%

Manganese - 2%

Zinc - 0.40%

Copper - 0.10%

Boron - 1.30%

Molybdenum 0.06%

I wish you the best of luck when making your own nutrient solution for the first time! Remember to wait for the solution to cool down before using it within your system.

Managing Varying Concentration and pH Levels

Over time the nutrient solution that you use will change in terms of concentration and pH level. I recommend that you use a digital Parts Per Million (PPM) meter that measures the concentration of salts in your solution. You can then compare the PPM concentration and continuously re-measure in order to keep the concentration of your solution as consistent as possible. This ensures your plant is able to continue extracting what it requires. The pH level of the solution also impacts a plants ability to absorb nutrients. An optimal pH level for plants is generally between 6.0 and 6.5, and to achieve this consistently you can utilize a readily available and affordable pH test and control kit. Easy to follow instructions will be provided with all kits.

By taking the time and effort to carefully control the

concentration and pH levels of your nutrient solutions, you will reap the benefits of having plants that grow more consistently and predictably.

Controlling Water Microbes

Another obstacle with keeping your nutrient solution effective is ensuring that the water remains sterile. Harmful anaerobic microbes can occur in your water which offsets the chemical/biological equilibrium in your nutrient solution - this can cause damage to the root systems of your plants. These microbes are likely to appear when water is warm and still, and will be evident from bad smells and brown roots.

To best prevent bad microbes I recommend maintaining the water's temperature between 68-75 degrees Fahrenheit, along with using a pump to regularly move the water around your system. This promotes oxygen and in turn good bacteria (aerobic microbes) that can fend off the bad anaerobic microbes. In order to monitor and regulate the temperature of the water in your solution, I simply suggest using an inexpensive aquarium thermometer.

Now that we've covered how to develop nutrient solutions to promote optimal plant growth, you will next be learning the importance of lighting for the growth of your plants and how you can create efficient lighting for your hydroponic configuration.

Section 5: Your Perfect Lighting Solution

"A big tree seemed even more beautiful to me when I imagined thousands of tiny photosynthesis machines inside every leaf."

— **Cynthia Kenyon**

Lighting plays a crucial role for plant growth, and therefore will be an important part of your hydroponic growth system. Through a process called photosynthesis, plants convert light - which is from the sun in nature - into sugars that energize a plant's growth. This is a result of chlorophyll located in the leaf cells that uses light and combines this with carbon dioxide and water - the end result is sugar and oxygen that is metabolized and transformed into energy for growth.

This makes the quality of the light you use vital for the prosperity of your plants. What we must aim to do within our hydroponic setup is to emulate the light that the sun produces with an artificial light source. Let's explore how you can best achieve this to guarantee positive results.

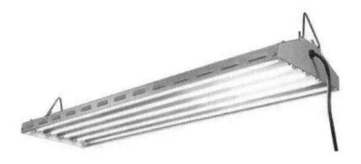

I strongly recommend using High Intensity Discharge (HID) Lighting for your growing efforts. It's widely agreed that this is a viable alternative to natural sunlight, and is certainly much more effective than the generic grow lights that you often come across. By providing the correct quality and amount of light, HID lighting has been specifically designed to produce the strongest photosynthesis reaction. And fortunately it's becoming increasingly accessible and affordable for the everyday hydroponic grower.

Intensity, Duration, and Color

For an optimal photosynthesis reaction, plants require 20-50 watts per square foot, depending on how much your chosen plants rely on light. Your HID lamp will have a wattage rating and this will determine the distance your lamp should have from your plants. Here is a general guide: 250Watt lamps should be approximately 12 inches from your plants, 400Watt lamps should be approximately 20 inches from your plants, and 1000Watt lamps should be at least 24 inches from your plants.

For maximum results, it's recommended to use paint in your growing area that has an eggshell finish - this increases the amount of light available for your plants. You can use a portable light meter to ensure your growing area is evenly lit throughout. Your plants will need different durations of light, depending on what you are growing - this is generally between 16 and 18 hours of light in a 24-hour time period.

Lastly, when choosing an HID lamp it's important to consider what spectrum of color they emit - this impacts levels of photosynthesis. If you will be growing leafy plants, it's best to use Metal Halide (MH) lamp that emits blue light. And if you decide to grow flowering plants, it is best to use a High Pressure Sodium (HPS) lamp.

Section 6: The Growing Process

"Growth is never by mere chance; it is the result of forces working together."

— James C. Penney (1875 - 1971)

Congratulations - you just about have the knowledge required to start the most important stage of hydroponics - the growing process! In this section we will be covering the ins and outs of the growing process to make sure you're well briefed for every step of the way. When you combine this knowledge with your own system (covered in the next section) you'll be quickly on your way to creating an impressive assortment of crops!

But before that, it's important to highlight that the conditions required will depend upon what type of plant you decide to grow. This is a good time to have a recap on the general requirements:

- Keep the temperature around the level that your plants require.

- Keep a moderate level of humidity.

- Use an effective source of lighting (covered in the last section).

- Provide plenty of fresh air to your plants for adequate levels of CO2.

- Provide oxygen to the root systems via a pump or agitation.

- Keep a consistent pH level (covered in section 4)

- Keep a consistent concentration of nutrient solution (covered in section 4).

For best results, I recommend doing specific research on the conditions require for your plant of choice, but here are some guidelines of favorable conditions for some popular choices:

Basil: High lighting, MH lamp, warm temperature.

Lettuce: Medium lighting, MH lamp, cool temperature.

Oregano: High lighting, MH lamp, warm temperature.

Parsley: High lighting, MH lamp, warm temperature.

Rosemary: High Lighting, 400/1000Watt lamp, warm temperature.

Strawberry: High lighting, 400/100Watt HPS lamp, warm temperature.

Tomato: High lighting, 400/100Watt HPS lamp, hot temperature.

Starting with Seeds

Seeds need to be started in a smaller separate area to your hydroponic system - when large enough, the plants will be transported to your main system.

The starting area should be a high humidity area with an appropriate starting medium. You can use a propagation tray along with a seed-warming mat to speed up germination.

To keep a high level of humidity you can use a dome over the propagation tray.

As a starting medium, starter sponges, coconut fiber, or Perlite produce good results (see section 2). The medium is then watered with a nutrient solution that is half the usual strength/concentration, and then kept moderately moist with the solution throughout the initial germination stage.

Below is a simple step-by-step process for successful seed starting:

1. Add moisture to your starting medium with half concentrated nutrient solution.

2. Insert seeds into the medium.

3. Ensure the temperature of the medium is between 72-80 degrees Fahrenheit.

4. Ensure the surrounding air is of a similar temperature.

5. Expose the area to soft light at first - increase this when the seeds have sprouted.

6. Keep the medium moderately moist with half strength solution throughout the starter stage.

Cloning From an Existing Plant

Another option you have is to start your growing process by making a clone from an existing plant. A growing tip is taken from another plant, and replanted so that it can form its own roots in the growing medium. This will then grow into a plant that is identical to the plant it was taken from.

If you opt for the cloning process, the same conditions are required for seeds but only a 25 percent concentration of nutrient solution is needed. Here is a simple process to get you started:

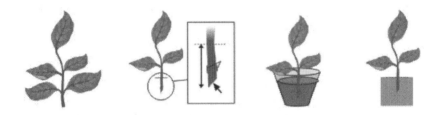

1. Select a healthy and green stem cutting from the plant of your choice - this should be approximately 3 to 5 inches.

2. Cut the tip off the plant using a clean and sharp knife.

3. Dip the tip into diluted nutrient solution.

4. Make another 45 degree cut from the initial cut.

5. Dip into a cloning root gel and then immediately into your starter sponge or medium.

The cutting now needs to be exposed to similar conditions to those of starting with seeds. The roots of the cuttings will develop within 1 to 3 weeks, after which they can be transferred into your main hydroponic medium.

Transplanting Into the Main System

Once your seeds or cuttings have formed a noticeable root system, it is time to move them over to your hydroponic system. This is easiest with starter sponges - simply remove and insert the plugs into your main growing medium and you will be good to go. But if you're using looser starting mediums I recommend using basket liners to make the process much smoother.

Once they have been carefully transplanted with their roots embedded into the medium, provide them with a lower than normal light exposure. This light intensity can then be increased after 3 to 4 days.

Now by putting into practice everything you have learned about creating a perfect growing environment, you will be on your way to having your own charming selection of crops.

Section 7: Creating Your Own Hydroponic System

"It takes half your life before you discover life is a do-it-yourself project."

— **Napoleon Hill (1883 - 1970)**

Where you decide to build your hydroponic system should depend upon how much space you have available. If growing indoors is more feasible for you, it's important to consider the availability of sunlight, and if possible use an area with a south-facing window. If a window isn't available, you have the option of using an effective HID lamp (see section 5).

Of course the main benefit of growing outside is being able to utilize free and powerful sunlight! If you have the space to grow outdoors it's vital to consider the temperature fluctuations of the growing area. You will need to keep temperatures within consistent ranges as previously discussed. It's worth remembering that rainfall can affect the pH levels of your nutrient solution. Also, make sure any electrical wiring you use is safe for outdoor use.

Avoid the use of metallic parts in your system where possible and wash all parts with a 1/10 concentration of bleach before use - this is to remove any contaminants that could affect your plants.

Earlier on in the book we explored some popular systems to give you an idea of how they operate. We're now going to provide you with the instructions to build our favorite and most effective systems that you can build yourself.

1. The Simple Hydroponic Planter

This is an elementary system that is quick and straightforward to construct. It's ideal for growing lettuces, herbs, and small flowers. And it's best suited to indoor use - ideally on a windowsill.

Required parts:

- Plastic planter (27 x 12 x 10 inches) with a seal bottom
- 2500cc minimum power pump and air supply tube
- Small hydroponic air curtain that covers the length of the planter
- At least 28 liters of LECA growing medium

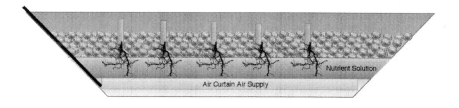

Steps to construct:

1. Secure the air curtain at the bottom of the planter.
2. Place the air pump supply tube along the bottom and up the side of the planter (this will be secured in place by the medium).
3. Fill the planter with water and turn on the pump to ensure it produces consistent bubble - empty the water afterwards.
4. Fill the planter with the LECA growing medium up to a couple of inches from the rim.
5. Pour in your nutrient solution of choice.
6. Insert your plants by making holes in the medium and inserting the roots as deep as possible.

Be sure that the plant roots are deep enough to be properly exposed to the nutrient solution beneath. Once this is all set up, turn on the air pump and your plants will now be on a rapid growth spurt!

2. The Raft System

This is another simple and effective system that is very affordable to construct - the other positive is that it generally takes less than 2 hours to build, depending on how handy you are!

As mentioned in section 3, this floating system is great for growing short term plants like lettuce. It can be used indoors, as well as outdoors if sheltered from rainfall.

Required Parts:

- Large reservoir container
- Air pump: single outlet
- Large rigid styrofoam sheet
- 2 inch net cups
- Air stone and air tubing
- LECA growing medium
- Starter sponges
- Nutrient solution

Tools required:

- Powered drill
- Hole saw slightly smaller than net cups or sharp razor knife
- Marker pen

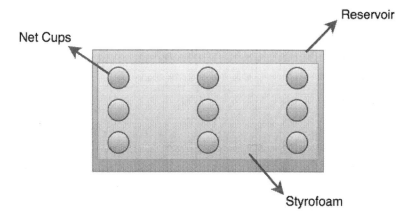

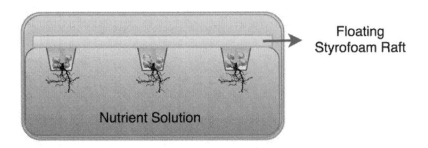

Floating
Styrofoam Raft

Nutrient Solution

Steps to construct:

1. Place the large container upside down on the styrofoam sheet and mark around the edge to create an exact outline of the container.
2. Cut the styrofoam slightly smaller than the outline to account for the distance between the outer and inner edge of the container. Make trimmings until the styrofoam sheet fits in and out of the container freely.
3. Mark holes in rows in the styrofoam using the net cups. I suggest using 3 holes per row.
4. Using a circular saw or sharp razor knife, cut the circular shapes out of the styrofoam and ensure the net cups fit comfortably into them.
5. Drill a hole the size of your air tube at the bottom of the side wall of the container. Insert a grommet into the hole.
6. Insert the air tube and attach this to the air stone.
7. Place the growing medium and the starter sponges in the net cups. Place these securely into the styrofoam holes.
8. Finally, fill the container with nutrient solution and ensure the roots have contact with it.
9. Turn on your pump and your plants are good to go!

3. The Autopot Self-Watering System

As mentioned in section 3, this is an intelligent self-feeding system that uses gravity to its advantage. This is achieved by employing a 'SmartValve' that automatically irrigates a tray that the growing pots are submerged in when the nutrient solution in the medium falls below a specific level. As you can imagine, this makes nutrient management a breeze - once the system is set up, it runs completely passively whilst your crops rapidly grow!

Autopots are pre-made systems that you can purchase - a typical system includes the following main components:

- Autopots and trays
- Reservoir
- Tubing
- Components to connect the pots to a nutrient feeding line
- A SmartValve feeder

Although autopot systems are bought pre-made, there are still customizations you can make to scale your growing process. For the best growing efficiency, I recommend using multiple autopots (3 or more) and connecting these via a feeding line to a large raised reservoir (over 40 gallons). The height of the reservoir will fully utilize the force of gravity - this allows you to grow a large group of plants with minimal effort. See below for an example system that you could set up with a number of autopots:

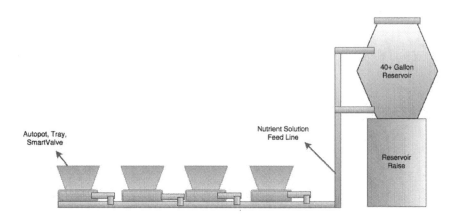

4. Indoor Hydroponic System

If you don't have the space or suitable conditions to grow outdoors, there is always the option to start your own hydroponics system in a spare closet! All you will need is one of the systems we've covered - combine this with an HID lamp and adhere to all the growing conditions that we explored earlier in the book (i.e. correct humidity, temperature etc). This will allow you to enjoy fresh homemade produce at all times of the year!

As an example, I recommend setting up the autopot system within a closet that has ample room for the autopots and a reservoir of at least 5 gallons. The nutrient reservoir will only need to be replaced every 5 days or so. Here's a diagram to give you an idea of what you could create in a previously useless closet of yours.

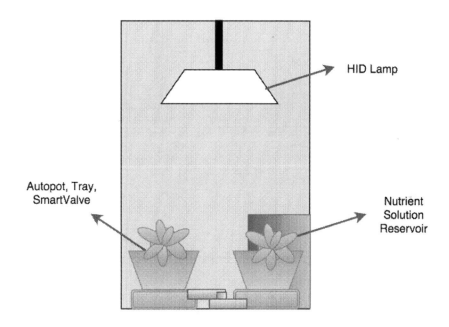

There's also the option to utilize an existing greenhouse that you have or have one constructed specifically for your hydroponic venture. This is of course a way to create excellent conditions for the range of plants you decide to grow.

The main benefit that growing in a greenhouse is that you can create ideal growing conditions which allows you to grow and produce fresh crops all year round! On top of this, a greenhouse is able to protect your crops from unwanted pests and diseases. Some of the most popular crops that are grown in greenhouses are lettuce, tomatoes, herbs, cucumbers, and peppers. Depending on what you choose to grow, any hydroponic system can be incorporated into a greenhouse. Not only will a greenhouse benefit the growth of your plants, but it can also be an uplifting tropical experience - somewhere you can retreat to in the midst of winter! If you are keen to set up a greenhouse for your growing, there are a number of considerations to make when creating the perfect environment.

Lighting

A great advantage of the greenhouse is that you are able control both the amount and quality of light with far more precision than when growing indoors in your home. A greenhouse is exposed to high quality natural sunlight which is of course optimal for plant growth. Even if there is less natural light over the winter months, additional artificial lighting can be introduced by means of HID lighting (see section 5). The amount of light required depends on the size of your greenhouse: as a general guide, you will need approx. 25 watts of lighting for each square foot of growing area in your greenhouse.

Temperature

It is important to remember that the temperature in a greenhouse will vary as a result of the weather outside. It will also depend on the insulation covering that you place on the exterior of your greenhouse. A very effective covering material is polyethylene which reduces heat loss from the greenhouse. That said, it important to note that polyethylene will need to be replaced every 3 years or so. You will need to develop a process of heating and cooling to control the temperature of your greenhouse. When heat enters the greenhouse via sunlight, it will get trapped and be unable to escape - this can cause the temperature to rise above the optimal level. Ventilation will need to be provided to cool the temperature back down to an appropriate level. This is particularly crucial during the summer months. Ventilation and cooling can be provided by using exhaust fans, and possibly cooling pads.

During the colder months, heating will be needed when there is a lack of sunlight. Space heaters will provide sufficient form of heat and these can be placed toward the roof of the greenhouse, or freestanding on the floor. Be sure to purchase an energy efficient space heater to keep your costs down.

Humidity

The optimal amount of humidity is approx. 75% for most crops. Levels of humidity that are too high can pose problems, and the best way to identify this is when there is visible moisture on the leaves of the plants. To reduce the humidity level you will need to replace the humid air with drier air by heating and exhausting the area. On the other hand, humidity levels may fall below optimal levels during the summer months when the air is dry. The best way to alleviate this is to utilize misters above your plants. These should be set to come in short bursts of 15 seconds every 15 to 20 minutes.

Section 8: Crops Most Suitable to Hydroponic Gardening

As mentioned earlier, you can grow virtually anything in your hydroponics garden. In this section I will cover the crops that I have had most success with, along with the different types and varieties best suited to hydroponic culture.

Arugula

There are two types of arugula that you can grow: rocket which is the standard salad arugula and wild arugula variants. A favorite wild rocket form is the Astro which is heat resistant and stronger in flavor. Both grow extremely well in hydroponic cultures.

Lettuce

There are a great variety of leaf lettuces that grow extremely well hydroponically. There is however one exception: the iceberg lettuce. This is because it needs colder temperatures in order to form a tight head. Iceberg lettuce is therefore not well suited to the backyard greenhouse setting. Besides this, iceberg lettuce has a very low nutritional value compared to other leafy greens.

The following are some favorite lettuce varieties:

Black Seeded Simpson: Many tend to start the season with this delicately flavored and tender leaf lettuce. This is because the Black Seeded Simpson is incredibly well suited to early spring sowing, yet is well adapted to a wide range of temperatures and climates.
For the best flavor, it is advised to harvest the lettuce early rather than late, once the leaves are large enough to use - as it grows to become more bitter and tough with time.

Winter density: This lettuce is compact, tightly folded with an excellent texture and flavor. Its leaves are dark green and it is well suited to all seasons.

Throughout the height of the season, I tend to enjoy different summer crisps. This is because summer crisps grow well, they don't build a bitter taste in the heat, and don't bold as easily as other varieties. Below are some favorites among the summer crisps:

Magenta: This summer crisp is shiny, puckered, has a great flavor and reddish leaves. Magenta is best suited to spring and summer sowing.

Muir: This summer crisp is the most heat tolerant lettuce. The leaves are light green, crisp and have an outstanding flavor.

Nevada: This lettuce has bright green leaves and is ideally suited to spring and summer sowing.

Lettuce Salad Mix

Instead of picking one particular lettuce type, you can also purchase your seeds in the form of lettuce mixes. These are premixed blends of different variants and colors of lettuce. You can create your own seed mix or opt for pre-mixed variants that are usually balanced for flavor, texture, and color. To create your own mix, you simply purchase the varieties of lettuce you wish to plant and mix them in a container prior to sowing.

The advantage of purchasing a pre-mixed blend is that all lettuce types in one mix are selected to have similar growth rates and uniform maturity. They can thus be harvested together. Johnny's Selected Seeds at www.johnnyseeds.com offers a great variety of premixed lettuce blends, my personal favorite being the 'Encore Lettuce Mix', a beautiful blend which includes Bibb lettuces, Green Oakleaf, Green Romaine, Lollo Rossa, Red Leaf, Red Oakleaf and Red Romaine.

Basil

Basil is a cooking staple, known for its outstanding aromas.
Basil leaves are flavorful and best when fresh. Because of
this, it is among the most favorite and sought-after herbs.

Italian basil

The most common basil we encounter is the Genovese, the
classic sweet Italian basil. Basil seeds germinate after around
5 – 10 days. The plant itself needs around 9 – 10 weeks to
reach maturity but can be harvested after 3 weeks.

For indoor hydroponics, it is recommended to use basil
plants that are Fusarium-resistant. Two examples of Italian
basils that are resistant to Fusarium include 'Nufa' and

'Aroma 2.'

Asian basils

Besides the Italian basil, there are also exotic types of basil that are commonly used in Thai and Vietnamese cuisines. Two varieties include 'sweet Thai', which grows to around 12 – 18 inches in height, and 'cinnamon' basils, which grow around 26 – 30 inches tall. Both variants take around 9 weeks to reach full maturity.

Greek basils

Greek basils, also called fine leaf basils, are most commonly used in pesto, stuffing, soup, and vegetable dishes. They have a stronger flavor than Italian basils. Two favorite Greek basils include 'pistou' which grow to around 6 – 8 inches in height, and the 'spicy bush' which grow 8 – 14 inches tall and take roughly 10 weeks to reach full maturity.

Citrus basils

There are also citrus basils that are often added to salads and fish dishes. They are favored for their distinct citrus aroma, take 8 – 9 weeks to reach maturity, and reach 20 – 24 inches in height.

Don't forget to trim!

To avoid basil from flowering or wooding, the plant needs to be cut every few weeks. Cutting also trains the plant to branch out and remain vegetative. If you see flowers, you should immediately cut these off to discourage wooding and to encourage your plant to become generative. Basil plants should be replaced after around 3 months.

Wait until your herb plant is around 6 inches tall or until it has around 3 - 5 sets of leaves before you start pruning (trimming) your plant. To trim your basil, cut the top off just above the second set of leaves, leaving at least two sets of side shoots below. As a general guideline, you should aim to trim your plant every 2 - 3 weeks, just above the first or second set of leaves of new branches, and pinch off any flowers as soon as you see them.

Basil plants grow quickly so don't hold back on pruning. Pruning in fact encourages growth. The more you prune your basil, the leafier and bushier it will become. You can use the pinched leaves straight away or dry them to use at a later date. Growing and cutting procedures are the same for all basils. All of these will grow extremely well in both NFT hydroponics systems and in a peatlite bed.

Herbs

Chervil

Chervil, or French parsley, is extremely well suited to hydroponic culture. It can be harvested for around 2 – 3 months once it reaches around 4 inches in height. Chervil germinates within 10 – 14 days. Like Basil, chervil should also be pruned to allow it to grow larger and bushier. In hot weather, the crop should be replaced after around 3 – 4 months.

Chives

There are two types of chives: regular fine leaf chives and garlic chives, also called Chinese leeks. Germination for both types is within 1 – 2 weeks. Fine leaf chives will continue to grow for a year without replacement and take around 10 – 12 weeks from sowing to the first harvest. Garlic chives take around 12 – 13 weeks from sowing to the first harvest. They can however be harvested as soon as they reach 6 – 8 inches in height. When harvesting however, make sure to leave around 3 inches of plant from the crown of the plant to stimulate re-growth. The flowers of garlic chives are edible and also make a beautiful garnish!

Coriander

Coriander is the edible seed of the plant known as 'cilantro'. Cilantro lend themselves extremely well to hydroponic cultures – they are slow to bolt and can also be grown as a micro green. Two of the best variants include 'Calypso' and 'Santo' which can be harvested as soon as they reach 12 – 18 inches in height (after roughly 7 – 8 weeks). Cilantro can be grown using either the nutrient film technique or plant towers. Like chervil, cilantro should be replaced after around 3 – 4 months. Cilantro takes 7 – 10 days for germination.

Dill

Dill can be harvested after 6 – 8 weeks and can reach around 40 inches in height once mature. To stimulate growth however, you can harvest it a little once it reaches around 8 – 10 inches in height, allowing at least 4 – 5 inches for regeneration. If you cut down your crop continuously every time it reaches around 8 – 10 inches in height, it should last for around 3 – 4 months. There are different types of dill. 'Verling' is an ornamental dill variant which can be used for cooking or as garnish. It grows around 42 – 48 inches tall. 'Fernleaf' is a dwarf dill variant which only reaches 26 – 32 inches in height. Fernleaf is best grown in plant towers. The seeds germinate within 2 – 3 weeks.

Fennel

Fennel matures after 7 – 8 weeks and grows around 24 – 36 inches tall. There are different fennel varieties, including 'Bronze' and 'Bronze and Green'. Fennel should be harvested on a regular basis once it reaches around 8 inches in height. Germination occurs within 1 – 2 weeks. This is because pruning will encourage growth for at least 3 – 4 months.

Lavender

Lavender is an all-time favorite that can grow to 12 – 30 inches in height. The crop takes around 14 – 16 weeks to flower and should be replaced after a year. If harvested for foliage, rather than for its purple flowers, harvest can begin once it reaches 8 inches in height. You should allow longer growth periods between harvests as the plant ages in order to avoid dieback.

Mint

Mint plants reach around 18 – 36 inches in height as they mature. They reach maturity within 8 – 9 weeks and can be harvested as soon as they grow 10 inches tall. Lavender germinates within 2 – 3 weeks. Provided they are pruned frequently, ideally every 3 weeks, they should last for a year before replacement is needed.

Oregano

Oregano is a must in on every pizza! The crop reaches around 8 – 24 inches in height over an 11 – 13-week period from sowing to full maturity. Germination occurs within 1 – 2 weeks. Harvesting can begin once the plant reaches around 8 inches in height. To stimulate continuous growth, it should be harvested every 3 weeks. Like mint, oregano plants will last for for around a year between crop changes, provided it is pruned regularly.

Parsley

Parsley will grow around 16 – 18 inches tall within an 11-week period. Harvest should begin as soon as the crop reaches 6 inches in height. Germination is slow and can take 2 – 4 weeks. To encourage continuous growth, it should be harvested every few weeks. Provided it is cropped regularly, it will last for around a year before a crop change is needed. When cutting back your parsley, make sure to leave at least 4 – 5 inches to avoid dieback. There are two main types of parsley. 'Forest Green' is a curled parsley, also referred to as moss parsley. 'Giant of Italy' is a flat leaf parsley that has large dark green leaves and grows strong and upright, and then hangs down as it matures.

Rosemary

Rosemary germination occurs within 2 – 3 weeks but can be irregular at times. The crop reaches maturity within 4 – 6 months. After 11 – 14 weeks, you can start cutting off the tips of the crop. Rosemary will grow for a year before a crop change is needed.

Sage

Sage reaches maturity at 11 – 13 weeks and can grow 16 – 30 inches long. But the crop can be harvested as soon as it reaches 6 inches in height. The seeds germinate within 1 – 3 weeks. Because sage hangs down, it is important to cut the crop on a regular basis. Regular trimming ensures that the plant remains succulent and productive for a year before a crop change is needed.

Thyme

Thyme is another culinary staple that can be harvested as soon as it reaches around 6 – 8 inches in length. The crop germinates in 3 – 4 weeks and can be harvested after approx.. 3 months. Thyme hangs and when fully grown, can reach a length of 6 – 12 inches. Thyme should be replaced after around 6 – 8 months. When harvesting thyme, cut straight across the shoots, leaving at least 4 inches of plant remaining for regeneration.

Trimming, Harvesting and Reducing Dieback

With all herbs, particularly if grown in a plant tower, regular pruning from the very beginning will reduce competition for light between plants. Regular pruning will also reduce dieback as well as keep the plant succulent and productive. If dieback occurs, remove the dead plant material as soon as possible to prevent cross-infection.

In order to harvest hanging herbs, take a handful, bunch them together, and use scissors and cut across them. It is important here to always leave at least 4 inches of growth (from the base of the plant to the cut) for regeneration. As the plant matures, leave at least 4 – 5 inches of growth when pruning. Don't allow the crop to flower unless your intention is to use them for scent or in floral arrangements. A plant should be changed once the interior of the bunch becomes dry and woody. Any dead plant material should be removed immediately to prevent infection.

To summarize, basil, chervil, coriander, dill, and fennel should be replaced after around 3 – 4 months. Thyme will need a crop change after around 6 months. Chives, lavender, oregano, parsley, rosemary and sage will, if regularly pruned, last for a year before a crop change is needed.

Vine Crops

Vine crops, such as eggplants, cucumbers, peppers and tomatoes, all have to be grown vertically with strings and support wires. While indeterminate varieties or staking plants can be grown indoors, they tend to perform best in greenhouses under a controlled environment. Using staking varieties requires substantial support but has the added benefit of making a better use of vertical space. Determinate varieties or bush plants are crop varieties that grow to a compact height. Bush plants require a limited amount of staking and will grow both indoors as well as in greenhouses, but they don't tend to yield as heavily as staking varieties.

Eggplants

- 'Agora', 'Berinda', and 'Taurus': These are purple high-yielding staking varieties that are designed for greenhouse growth include.

- 'Tango': This is a productive white eggplant of the staking variety.

There are many different 'bush' eggplants that come in different colors and shapes. These can also be grown hydroponically but are not as productive as the staking plants.

- 'Hansel': This is a purple eggplant of the bush variety. The plant is small, around 2 feet tall, and is therefore ideally suited to container growing.

- 'Fairy Tale': This is a purple eggplant with white strips that is tender, plump and sweet in taste. They are the same size as Hansel and are therefore also perfect for growing in containers.

Cucumber

There are many different cucumber varieties. Which variety you should choose will largely depend on growing conditions: temperature, humidity and light conditions.

The following varieties are resistant to Powdery mildew, a

fungus disease that affects a wide range of different plants, and tend to be best suited to humid conditions: 'Camaro', 'Dominica', 'Fidelo', 'Flamingo', 'Logica', and 'Marillo'. There are also many other varieties, including 'Bologna', 'Discover', and 'Optima.' Because of the wide range of different available varieties, it is recommended to try a few different verities and see which ones tend to perform best in your hydroponic garden. With cucumbers, it is best to change crop every 3 – 4 months to ensure you get the greatest yield.

Peppers

Pretty much all peppers will grow well hydroponically, whether indoors or in a greenhouse. It is again recommended to opt for the staking varieties in order to make best use of vertical space. Sweet bell peppers are the most popular pepper. The following are, in my experience, some of the most productive varieties:

Red peppers include:

- 'Fantasy': A large and heavy red pepper bell that is high-yielding with good shelf-life characteristics.

- 'Triple 5': A good-sized pepper that matures quickly with a high production level.

- 'Zamboni': A large and easy-to-grow plant variety which is extremely high yielding.

Orange peppers include:

- 'Arancia': A popular bell pepper with excellent fruit quality. Arancia is suitable for long term heated cultivations but can also be planted in unheated environments.

- 'Magno': Lobed and blocky, Magno is well suited for both non-heated and slightly heated cultivations.

- 'Sympathy': This pepper bell has a long shelf life and excellent fruit quality. It is also suitable for winter planting seasons.

Yellow peppers include:

- 'Amber': A sweet yellow-green bell pepper that is high yielding, particularly in a greenhouse environment. It is suitable for autumn, winter and spring cultivations.

- 'Bachata': A blocky yellow pepper that is well suited for heated greenhouse production but which also grows well in unheated environments.

- 'Striker': This bell pepper performs well under both high and low temperatures.

Tomatoes

There are many different types of tomatoes which generally fall within the following categories:

- 'Beefsteak' (200 – 250 grams): These are traditionally large fruits weighing up to 250 grams. Popular varieties include 'Beverly', 'Caiman', 'Caramba', Dombito', 'Matrix', 'Style', and 'Trust'.

- 'Cherry' (15 – 25 grams): These are small in size and sweet tasting. Popular varieties include 'Conchita' (red in color), 'Favorita' (red), 'Juanita' (red), 'Goldita' (yellow), and 'Zebrino' (red with green stripes).

- 'Cocktail' (30 – 75 grams): A popular variety being 'Red Delight'.

- 'Grape' or 'Plum' (15 – 25 grams): These are, like cherry tomatoes, small in size but slightly more oval in shape. Popular varieties include 'Dasher' (red), 'Flavorino' (red), 'Picolino' (red), 'Goldino' (yellow), and 'Orangino' (orange).

- Heirloom (20 – 30 grams): These are an indeterminate variety which are well suited for both greenhouse growing and indoor hydroponic cultures. Popular varieties include 'Brandywine' (red), 'Striped Green Zebra' (red with green stripes), and 'Yellow Pear' (yellow).

- 'Roma' (100 – 150 grams): Popular varieties include 'Granaderp', 'Naram', and 'Savantas'.

- 'Tomato-on-vine (TOV)' (90 – 150 grams): These tomatoes can be harvested individually but are mostly packaged as trusses of fruit. Popular varieties include: 'Ambiance', 'Clarance', 'Clermon', 'Grandela', 'Orangaro' (an orange variety), 'Tradiro', and 'Tricia'.

The majority of the tomatoes listed above can be harvested 10 – 11 weeks after sowing. They will grow for a year before a crop change is needed.

Section 9: Pest Prevention and Troubleshooting

"Prevention is better than cure."

— Desiderius Erasmus (1466 - 1536)

Unfortunately when growing anything there's a risk in encountering issues that hinder the quality of your plants. That being said, with hydroponics it's fairly simple to prevent such problems arising, which will ensure you get your desired results!

It's vital to keep your growing area free of pests, and you will more than likely achieve this if you keep the growing area very clean. However, pests have a higher chance of becoming a problem when you're growing indoors - there are fewer natural pest preventatives (e.g. rainfall, birds etc.), so it's even more crucial that you keep your indoor growing area obsessively clean. Make sure to remove any stray mud, dead leaves, or any other excess debris.

If you're still one of the unlucky ones, then here are some solutions for the main growing issues.

Fungi and Algae:

Too much humidity in your growing area can give rise to fungi growth. As mentioned throughout the book, it's critical that the correct humidity levels are maintained and your growing area is supplied with a constant supply of fresh air. You should also constantly remove any dead stems or leaves from the area, and avoid excessive watering of the plants. But if you're unfortunate enough to experience a fungi outbreak, using a quality fungicide will be a viable option to solve the issue. If you can spot an outbreak early enough then you'll have the chance to prevent further growth by carefully removing the fungi with a dry cloth.

It's important to be aware of other types of fungus that can become a problem on the growing medium. If you notice this then use a layer of LECA medium on the top layer of your existing medium - this will help absorb any excess moisture.

Algae is another potential difficulty that thrives from receiving light. This can occur both in your nutrient solution reservoir and on the growing medium - it will compete for nutrient solution which can deprive your plants. Be sure there aren't any direct rays of light entering your reservoir, and make sure the water is being regularly agitated. If this does occur significantly in your reservoir, it will need washing out with 1/10 concentration of bleach. If it occurs on the growing medium, be sure to completely wipe it away.

Pests:

Although we've already covered the preventative measures, we'll cover what you can do if you do end up with pests infesting your sacred plants. Many growers choose to use toxic pesticides - I don't recommend this as a number of bugs can develop resistance to them which can make them useless. My favorite natural solution is to use sticky traps that lure in pests with a bright color and then trap them, making them a pest no longer! These can be easily made by using petroleum jelly spread on top of a blue or yellow painted cardboard strip.

Overall, make sure that you're very meticulous in constantly checking your plants and growing area - this will give you the best chances of eliminating any potential threats before they become a full blown hindrance!

Conclusion: Last but Not Least

I'd like to take this opportunity to thank you for downloading this book. I hope you now have a solid foundation on the process, and that you're equipped with the knowledge to put you on the path to becoming a hydroponic hero!

My final piece of advice - no matter how diligent you are in your research, your best learning will come from *doing,* so don't hesitate in getting started. Start simple, perhaps with one of the basic systems outlined and with a easier crop such as lettuce and herbs. Once you put your knowledge into practice you'll soon have the skills to advance onto more challenging systems and growing vine and fruit plants. I recommend revisiting the sections along with careful further research to constantly refresh your knowledge as you progress.

I sincerely wish you the best of luck in your hydroponic venture.

Best wishes,

Andy Jacobson

Bonus: Starting a Hydroponics Business

As a keen gardener, what would be better than being able to do what you love, produce beautiful crops, and also make a profit from it! If this is something that you are interested in pursuing, with the right plan and mindset it's certainly something that you can achieve. Below are the key considerations you should make when planning to start a business from your hydroponic venture.

Check Your Local Demand and Market

The first thing you will need to determine is who would potentially be interested in buying your produce. Both local restaurants and markets are often looking for new suppliers of high quality produce. By investigating this market you will start to gain an idea of what is in demand and what you should grow. I suggest physically going out to communicate with restaurants and markets to identify some unique opportunities. It is always best to try pinpoint products that have a strong and stable demand - this will allow you to set a good price point. A prime example of this would be herbs such as basil. Fresh basil is always on the radar of good restaurants and it should be fairly straightforward to get interest for this culinary herb. On top of this, herbs require fairly little growing space and therefore easy to grow at large volumes - giving you a plentiful supply to fill the local demand!

At this stage it's also important to start looking into the legal requirements for starting a business in your area. This will likely prevent any administrative headaches in the future.

When exploring your local market start examining the selection of fresh herbs available, along with the level of the quality. Surprisingly enough, you will often many herbs that are below the standard that you could offer. It's a good idea to take note of both the quantities that are being sold and the pricing. Be sure to do conduct this informal research at a number of establishments, and you will then be able to compile this information to work out averages.

As I suggest starting your business with herbs, here is a list of some of the herbs that generally have the best demand and can be sold for a profitable price:

- Basil

- Oregano

- Mint

- French Tarragon

- French Sorrel

- Rosemary

- Dill

- Parsley

- Chive

- Sage

- Thyme

The Quality of Your Product

The most important factor for determining the success of your business is product quality. The great thing is that by growing hydroponically you can ensure that the quality of your products are top quality. I strongly suggest taking some time to perfect your hydroponic technique until you are able to get high quality results that are consistent. When you win your first clients, they will expect consistent results, and if you can deliver this your brand loyalty keep growing. On top of the quality of your produce, you will need to consider how your present your product. You will need to create product packaging that reflects the quality of your produce. As the saying goes, 'less is more' and you don't necessarily need sophisticated packaging - it is best to keep your costs down in the initial stages. You can simply use basic ziplock plastic bags with a sharp and clean label with your brand on. Make sure you make discreet breathing holes and apply a mist to your herbs before packaging them to maximize freshness.

Branding, Branding, Branding

For long term success it is very important to develop a 'brand' for your business. You want your brand name to be recognizable to your current and prospective customers. Ultimately, you want quality to be associated with your brand which will help expand your business into more markets. People will already be aware of your product quality and will be keen to give you their money over another producer who has not established themselves with a brand.

Providing Samples to Prospective Customers

Once you are happy with your produce and branding, it is now time to make an introduction to local traders. Firstly, package up some samples of produce with your branded label, and placing these in a cooler with ice to keep the products as fresh as possible. You can then start by approaching smaller establishments and tracking down the buyer or owner. Once you are able to get in front of the right person by asking to have a quick meeting to discuss your high quality produce, simply present them with some of your fresh samples. Explain your process of growing hydroponically and emphasize the fact that you never use chemical pesticides and herbicides. On top of this, be sure to make clear that the high quality of your produce is a result of your crops being provided with a constant supply of quality nutrients and water. If at this stage there is interest, let them know that you are a local producer which should further increase their interest.

If you are able to, get your contact to taste your product as soon as possible. This is often the critical factor in gaining a strong interest and desire for your product. Remember, your product is likely of much higher quality in terms of appearance and taste than any of the current suppliers they are using. Make a proposition of running a trial of selling your produce in their market. If they are interested enough to make a financial investment in your product then that is brilliant. However, if they are slightly reluctant it is likely that you will be able to come to an agreement on a consignment basis, i.e. they will put your products on sale and only pay you when the product sells. I recommend working on a consignment where they pay you 50% of their selling price, this may well be slightly higher than your competitors you can negotiate this as being fair due to your higher growing costs and better product quality. Hopefully you will get an agreement at this stage and you can move onto working out the logistics of supply and delivery!

Once you have locked in with one reseller, ensure you are constantly monitoring the market. This should involve regularly visiting the market so see what is selling well and ensuring you are providing an abundance of supply. In order to scale your business, it is time to reach out to new dealers and win their business. You will now be more confident and will have already started to build some brand recognition, so it should be a breeze to win some new business. Keep a close relationship with local merchants, they will always be interested in working alongside you - when you make profit they make profit!

Overall, by following the outlined steps and adding a twist of your own entrepreneurial spirit, you will certainly be able to build a stable and lucrative business. Whether you want a small side venture to pay your bills each month, or a full-time business that supports your family, the opportunities are waiting for you!

Bonus

The Essential Aquaponics Guide

A Step-By-Step Aquaponics Gardening Guide To Growing Vegetables, Fruit, Herbs, and Raising Fish at the Same Time

Andy Jacobson

Foreword

"To plant a garden is to believe in tomorrow."

- **Audrey Hepburn (1929 – 1993)**

Aquaponics captured my interest and fascination the first time I heard about this farming tradition and the theory that underpins it. In my eyes, the most beautiful aspect of aquaponics is that it mirrors nature in its harmonious self-sufficient eco-cycles. This innovative production process is something I wish to share with you. Water is what keeps ecosystems thriving and is essential to our very existence. Water is the foundation of life. Sadly, and worryingly, water scarcity is a profound and imminent problem in today's world. Because of all this, the use of recycled water in aquaponics has never been more attractive.

Motivated by the potential to make food security a priority and frugal living a possibility, I am thrilled to take you on an aquaponic voyage – from guiding you through how to build your own fully-sustainable aquaponic garden to breaking down the science into concise, proven steps on how to yield the best results. This easy-to-follow guide is carefully tailored toward hobby gardeners as well as more advanced explorers of urban homesteading.

For your best understanding and results, I recommend

reading this book in the order it has been structured with. This essential aquaponics guide will cover the following: An introduction to aquaponics, how it works and its benefits, the best plants and fish to use, aquaponic system designs, how to assemble, cycle and maintain your aquaponic garden, and much more! All information will be presented with clear explanations, reference pictures and diagrams. This DIY guide will give you all the tools you need to create your own aquaponic Eden which will provide you with fresh and organic greens all year round.

By the end of the book, you will be able to create your own customized aquaponic garden by choosing and combining some of the systems and growing options we supply, depending on your food growing goals.

The ultimate goal? To allow you to grow your own food from the comfort of your own home whilst paving your path to a frugal, self-sustaining lifestyle.

Best Wishes,

Andy Jacobson

Section 1: An Introduction to Aquaponics

"The home gardener is part scientist, part artist, part philosopher, part ploughman. He modifies the climate around his home."
- John R. Whiting

What is Aquaponic Gardening?

Aquaponics is a revolutionary, highly effective gardening system which combines conventional aquaculture (raising aquatic animals in tanks) with hydroponics (cultivating plants in soil-free media). In a symbiotic environment, it raises both fish and plants in mutual ecological harmony. Like Hydroponics, the aquaponic growing methods don't require any soil and instead make use of highly oxygenated, nutrient-rich water.

Aquaponic gardening is highly productive in growing organic vegetables, herbs, fruits and raising fish. More so, aquaponic systems are four to six times more productive than ordinary gardens and require 90% less water. On a small scale, they provide a cost-efficient alternative to families and anyone seeking self-sufficiency. On a larger scale, they are a potential solution to urban food insecurity.

Not only is aquaponics among the most effective gardening

techniques, but it is the easiest way to grow herbs and vegetables. Aquaponic systems are self-regulating: you don't have to water your plants and you don't have to clean the fish tank. Aside from some simple maintenance tasks (which we will outline in *Section 10*), the only thing left to do is to feed your fish and harvest your vegetables!

The Aquaponic Cycle: How It Works

Put simply, as water is pumped from the fish tank to the grow beds, the fish waste is converted to organic food for your plants. Your plants in turn clean, filter and recycle the water for your fish. Because aquaponics is a closed and recirculating system, it gives rise to naturally occurring bacteria (microbes and worms). These bacteria and worms break down the fish waste (ammonium and nitrites) into fertilizer for your plants (in the form of nitrites).

When absorbing these nutrients, plants naturally filter the water. The clean water then streams back into the aquarium, providing your fish with a clean and oxygenated environment in which they can thrive.

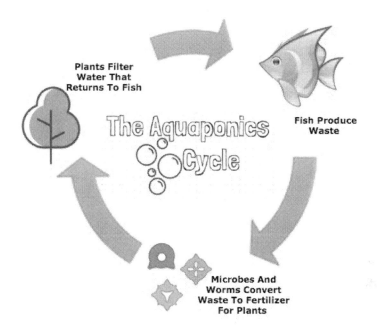

Plants Filter
Water That
Returns To Fish

The Aquaponics
Cycle

Fish Produce
Waste

Microbes And
Worms Convert
Waste To Fertilizer
For Plants

This growing method is environmentally-friendly, natural and economical. Using natural bacterial cycles, it eliminates all need for expensive chemical fertilizers and water filters, all whilst avoiding waster wastage.

We will expand on the many benefits of aquaponics in the next section, before moving on to how you can get started on your journey to self-sufficiency and food independence!

Section 2: The Benefits of Aquaponic Gardening

"The destruction of aquatic ecosystem health, and the increasing water scarcity, are in my opinion the most pressing environmental problems facing human kind."

- Maude Barlow

Sustainable Aquaculture:

In aquaponic cycles, the same water is used to raise both fish and plants. Fish waste is used as fertilizer to grow agricultural products. Plants in turn filter and recycle the water, thereby cleaning the fish tank and allowing your fish to thrive. This makes aquaponics one of the most waste-efficient, water-saving and most natural farming systems.

Low Maintenance and Greater Yields:

Because aquaponics mimics the natural ecosystem, maintenance requirements are extremely low when compared to other agricultural systems. There is no ploughing, tilling, mulching or weeding to do. Apart from feeding your fish and some simple maintenance checks, there is not much else to do other than to harvest your produce. You will find more on maintenance in *section 10* of this guide, where we will outline the daily, weekly and monthly checks and tasks recommended to keep your system healthy.

Despite lower maintenance requirements, aquaponics is among the most efficient growing methods. Aquaponics is said to be 4-6 times more productive than traditional farming.

For Health Reasons:

When compared to traditional agricultural farming, aquaponics is both safer and much cleaner. On top of this, aquaponic gardening is completely organic! The dangers of pollution, pesticides and other risks associated to the use of chemicals is greatly reduced as well. Furthermore, because the plants are not grown in soil, this eradicates all risks of soil-borne diseases and weeds.

For Environmental Reasons:

Modern aquaponics uses a small amount of freshwater and little energy. Although aquaponic gardening does require some energy (to power the pumps), this is significantly less when compared to soil-based farming. Modern agriculture is a massive contributor to climate change. Other overuse of petroleum use in traditional farming is vast and the consequences devastating. Because aquaponic systems are soil-free, this removes the need for tractors and other farming equipment. In addition to this, there is also no need for petroleum-based fertilizer nor chemical pesticides in aquaponic gardening.

More importantly, because aquaponics is a closed and recirculating system, there is virtually no water wastage.

Self-sufficiency:

Once your system is fully cycled (a process explained in *Section 9* of this guide), it is extremely sustainable and self-sufficient. You are not dependent on arable land nor restricted by climate. Productive and fertile soil is a nonrenewable and endangered ecosystem. In aquaponics, there is no soil to show tiredness and which might be at risk of erosion and degradation.

Not only is aquaponics therefore the ideal solution for the urban gardener, but also for communities that live on non-fertile land. In a global context, aquaponic gardening therefore provides a potential solution to food shortages around the world.

Organic Fish:

Furthermore, buying sustainably grown and harvested fish today, is a difficult undertaking. Being able to grow your own fish is thus a more convenient, more ecological; a fresher and safer alternative.

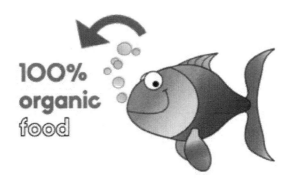

Aquaponics vs Hydroponics

Aquaponics, essentially, is a hydroponic growing technique in that it requires no soil. Both are highly efficient methods for growing plants which achieve results that are greater than those found in soil-based gardening. In many ways however, aquaponics is an improvement to hydroponics. Fish waste replaces expensive chemical nutrients and there is no need to throw away your nutrient solution. Additionally, once your aquaponic bio-filter is fully established (usually after six months), aquaponics is said to produce greater and faster-growing plants when compared to hydroponics.

Now that we have a sound understanding of the many benefits of aquaponic gardening and it potential impact locally and globally, this is now a great time to start considering the different types of hydroponic systems that are possible.

Section 3: The Design of Your Aquaponic Unit

"One of the most delightful things about a garden is the anticipation it provides."

- W.E. John (1893 – 1968)

In this section, I will explain the essential elements of your aquaponic garden. This is to give you a general idea of the outline and possible designs of aquaponic systems. Later on in the guide, I will discuss the importance of sizing and ratios, as well as how to assemble and construct your own aquaponic unit.

Let's begin with the outline of the basic flood and drain system before explaining how you can advance your system with time.

For Hobby Growers:

Flood and Drain

The flood and drain system is among the easiest systems to assemble. When starting to build your aquaponic garden, I would always recommend to start with a 1:1 ratio between the grow bed and the fish tank. In other words, try and select a grow bed that mirrors your fish tank in volume size.

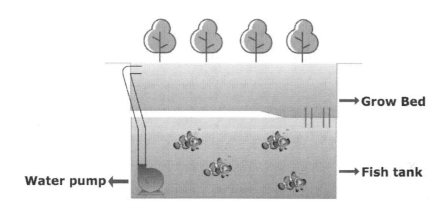

How it works:

- The grow bed is raised above the fish tank.
- Water is pumped from the fish tank into the grow bed.
- The plants filter and recycle the water.
- The clean water flows back into the fish tank through the draining pipes as a result of gravity.

Water movement is central to the health of your system. As a general rule, try and cycle the water of your system twice every hour. For example, if your system contains a volume of water which is 1000 liters, the rate at which your water flows should be 2000 liters/hour.

After 4 to 6 months...

While your fish are still small and are producing relatively little waste, I would recommend sticking to one grow bed. But once your system has matured (after 4-6 months) and your fish have grown, you may wish to add another grow bed.

Achieving the 'flood and drain' effect

There are two ways in which you can create the flood and drain effect. In both plumbing systems, the pump is located in the fish tank. The first option is to have a standpipe in the grow bed alongside a timer on the pump. Alternatively, you can use an auto siphon in the grow bed along with a continuous pump.

We will explore more deeply how these plumbing systems work and how you can set them up in *Section 8* of this book, where we will will provide you with a shopping list as well as a step by step guide to building your very own aquaponic system.

For the Ultimate Garden Guru

The CHIFT PIST System

You might also be interested in the following more complex aquaponic set-up.

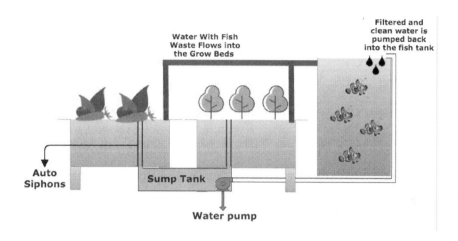

This system design is called CHIFT PIST, which stands for 'constant height in fish tank, pump in sump tank.'

How it works:

- Water from the grow beds flows into the sump tank by the force of gravity.
- This recycled water is pumped into the fish tank either continuously or periodically by the pump located in the sump tank. For periodic pumping, you can install a float switch which will activate your pump once the water in the sump tank has reached a certain level.

- Water from the fish tank flows into the grow beds as a result of gravity through an overflow pipe. Because of this, the fish tank will remain at a constant water level.
- Water level in the grow beds are controlled by auto-siphons, which drain excess water into the sump tank.

Which of the above system you choose will depend on a number of factors: If you wish to keep it relatively small-scale, I would highly recommend the basic flood and drain system. If you wish to grow more vegetables and are concerned about saving energy, the CHIFT PIST system should definitely be the one to go for.

In the next section, we will explore the different available mediums that you can use in your aquaponics system as a substitute to soil. We will then delve into the different fish species and plants species that are well suited to aquaponics.

Section 4: Media-based Aquaponics

There are other aquaponic systems that exist, for example the raft system (deep-water culture), as well as the Nutrient Film Technique (NFT). Please note that this guide will only cover media-based aquaponics for multiple reasons.

A key reason why I only cover the media-based approach is that this is the only system which allows you to grow the greatest variety of plants. In the raft system for example, only small leafy vegetables can be grown. Alongside greater flexibility and greater choice, the media-based system is the most frugal, energy-efficient set-up, and the one which also requires the least maintenance. Because of this, media-based aquaponics is the single most suited system for backyard aquaponics and, in my opinion, even for commercial growers.

The Media-filled Bed Method

A media-filled bed is a vegetable bed filled with 'growing media.' The media, in many ways, replaces soil and its purpose. Functionally, the media acts as a filter as well as coat, protecting roots from rapid changes in temperature, otherwise detrimental. Structurally, the media acts as a platform for CO_2/H_2O exchange, and as a home for worms. Worms?

Yes, the secret to these vegetable beds are red worms; also called red wigglers. These red wigglers are composting worms which do a tremendously great job in breaking down the solids in the vegetable bed, keeping your garden clean and tidy. On top of this, red wigglers also create fertilizer – providing additional food to your plants.

Selecting the ideal media:

There is a variety of requirements when it comes to selecting the right media. Among the most important are that they don't decompose, are resistant to changes in pH and also the correct size. Media that is too small becomes clogged whilst media that is too big creates air pockets which are not favorable to your plants.

Below is a list of media I have used and recommend, and which also fulfil all of the above requirements:

Expanded Shale: This is acquired from quarries. Expanded Shale is pH neutral with round edges and therefore easy to handle and also good for your plant roots.

Expanded Clay (Hydroton): Like Expanded Shale, Expanded Clay is also mined from a quarry, pH neutral and easy to handle.

River stone: River stone is heavy but easy to handle. Please note however that river stone is the riskier option. If your batch contains limestone, this could raise the pH levels in your growing bed, which would make the grow media unsuitable to your aquaponic system. To test whether it contains limestone, rinse your stone and place it in a cup of vinegar. If you can observe fizzing bubbles coming to the surface, don't use it.

The same test can be used on gravel. Although gravel is also one of the cheapest options, it's not one that I would personally recommend. If you do however opt for gravel, please make sure it doesn't contain any limestone or marble.

Synthetic media: Synthetic media is made from petroleum and is pH neutral and very light. Synthetic media has the ideal qualities for an aquaponic media grow bed, however, it tends to be more expensive compared other grow medias.

Whichever media you choose, make sure to thoroughly wash it before using it in your system! Now that you have a general knowledge of the mediums that can be used to support the growth of your plants, in the next section it's time to learn everything you need to know about fish!

Section 5: Fish: Selecting, Purchasing and Breeding

"Growing your own food is like printing your own money."

- Ron Finley

Selecting the Right Fish for You

When selecting your fish beware that you must use freshwater fish only. This is because extended exposure to sodium in salt water is not an ideal environment for your plants.

Below are a list my favorite fish as they are very well suited to be raised in an aquaponic garden. Please note however that it is advised to stick to one fish type per tank because different fish are best suited to specific water qualities:

- Tilapia
- Goldfish
- Perch
- Catfish
- Peruvian Pacu
- Oscars
- Trout
- Koi
- Freshwater prawns

Of course, there are many other options open to you, including barramundi and even freshwater lobster!

For beginners and anyone taking their first dive into aquaponics, I would highly recommend Tilapia and Goldfish, depending whether you wish to raise fish for food or not. Both fish produce very high levels of ammonia, providing your plants with a lot of organic food. Both fish are also extremely resilient to changes in temperature, pH levels and pollutants.

Tilapia are the most frequently used fish in aquaponics and there is a reason for this! I highly recommend this fish due to the qualities they possess. Not only are Tilapia easy to breed, they are also among the fastest growing fish and can tolerate and survive in very poor water conditions.

For vegetarians and gardeners not interested in breeding but rather in raising beautiful fish, I would recommend both koi and goldfish. These are both ornamental fish that are at the same time well-suited to aquaponics. If you're not too fussed about which fish to choose, I would suggest you start with goldfish. Goldfish are easy to grow and easily acquired. On top of this, they tolerate a wide range of temperatures and conditions, produce good waste for your plants and also live comfortably in small aquariums.

When deciding which fish you choose, the following are key

factors to take into account:

Stock density: The size of your aquarium will affect the size of fish that is best suited to your aquaponic garden. As a general guide, you can grow approximately 500g of fish for every 5 to 7 gallons of fish tank water.

Edible vs ornamental: As previously discussed, your choice of fish will depend on whether or not you seek to raise fish for food.

Water temperature: Different fish have different temperature requirements. We will outline the temperature requirements of the most popular fish later on in this section.

Oxygen requirements: Certain fish will survive in low quality water, that is, water with low oxygen levels. However, highly oxygenated water will allow your fish to thrive. More on oxygen requirements of your fish later on in this section.

Carnivore vs Omnivore:

Whichever fish you choose; they will have specialized feeding needs. Beware to keep the diet of your fish in mind when selecting which fish species to opt for.

However, don't worry too much about which fish to raise – you can always change your mind at a later stage!

Purchasing your fish:

When purchasing your fish, these are a few tips and tricks to keep in mind. First of all, the most cost-efficient way to acquire fish is by purchasing fingerlings. Fingerlings are small young fish, which are both inexpensive and easily transportable. Don't worry if you don't live near a fish farm as there are also many hatcheries that sell online.

The ideal environment for your fish:

Remember that different fish have different requirements which is dependent on their natural habitat.

To make your fish selection process easier, I have included the fish requirements of some of my favorite fish below. It is important to bear in mind that fish will reach their highest metabolic rates in their most comfortable temperature and thus provide most fertilizer to your plants when kept in their 'optimal' environment. Keeping fish in the right temperature is also best for their immune system which directly affects their life cycles as well as the health of your plants.

<u>Edible fish</u>

Tilapia:

Tilapia originate from the waters of Africa and therefore thrive most in warm waters. Their optimal temperature is 74 – 80 °F, although they can tolerate temperatures ranging from 60 – 95 °F. Furthermore, Tilapia naturally live in ponds and lakes. Because of this, they are used to relatively low quality of water and limited amounts of oxygen and can therefore survive in environments which would generally be considered less than favorable.

Catfish:

Their optimal temperature is 75 – 85 °F, although they can tolerate temperatures ranging from 35 – 95 °F. Like Tilapia, Catfish originate from ponds and lakes and can also survive in low oxygenated, low quality water. However, as a general rule of thumb, all fish do best in water with great amounts of oxygen.

Trout:

Trout originate from North America and therefore prefer colder water. Their optimal temperature is 55 – 65 °F, although they can tolerate temperatures ranging from 35 – 68 °F. Because trout hail from streams and mountain rills, they are best adapted to water high in oxygen.

Another important factor to keep in mind is that trout are carnivores and thus require a high-protein diet. To sustain this, I would advise to purchase commercial fish food of high quality and nutrition. When dealing with carnivorous fish, it is likewise recommended to only keep fish of approximately the same size together in a tank. This will save your smaller fish from being eaten by their big brothers.

Ornamental fish

Goldfish:

Their optimal temperature is 65 – 75 °F, although they can tolerate temperatures ranging from 35 – 95 °F. As goldfish are routinely kept in ponds, they too, can survive in low quality water with limited amounts of oxygen.

Koi:

Their optimal temperature is 65 – 75 °F, although they can tolerate temperatures ranging from 35 – 95 °F. Like goldfish, Koi can also live in waters with lower levels of oxygen. Unlike goldfish however, Koi can prove slightly harder to source. It is advised to consult a specialty aquarium shop as well as to explore the many koi variations available.

Feeding your fish:

Be careful not to overfeed your fish. A good indication as to how much food to feed your fish is to feed your fish as much as they can eat within 5 minutes.

If your fish aren't eating, this can be a sign of stress either due to a lack of oxygen or because the water temperature is outside their optimal range.

Before we move on to the best plants to grow in your aquaponic garden, it is important to note the dangers of temperature swings. Although fish can tolerate varying temperatures, fast changes in temperature should be approached with caution. If you experience temperature changes of more than 3 – 4 °F within 24 hours, it is advised to *immediately* stop feeding your fish. This is because temperature swings can cause gut bacterial problems that may be fatal to your beloved fish.

Now that we have covered the different fish species well suited to aquaponic systems and their optimal environments, it is time to explore the plant species which will guarantee you the greatest success on your aquaponic journey!

Section 6: Picking the Best Plants

"Gratitude for the seemingly insignificant – a seed – this plants the great miracle."

- Ann Voskamp

To give you an idea of the range of produce you can grow, the following is a list of plants which are commonly grown and which are known to flourish and respond exceptionally well to aquaponic gardening:

- Salads (everything from lettuce to spinach)
- Herbs (including basil, parsley, watercress, coriander, sage, lemongrass)
- Chives
- Broccoli
- Cauliflower
- Tomatoes
- Peppers
- Egg plant
- Choy
- Cucumbers
- Beans and peas
- Squash
- Melons
- Strawberries

Beyond these possibilities, the variety of plants you can grow is even greater! So what can't you grow in your aquaponic system? The only plants you cannot grow are those that require a pH level beyond your optimal range. Aquaponic systems only support a pH of 6.8 – 7 (more on pH and how to control and change pH levels in *Section 9*). Blueberries for example, which require very acidic soil, are not well suited to aquaponics. The list of acid-loving vegetables and fruits however, is very small and hardly restricts the variety you can grow.

Timing:

In any case, I would recommend starting with lettuce and other leafy greens as they have relatively low nutrient requirements. This means that they are best supported and will still successfully grow in developing aquaponic systems. This is because fingerlings will produce relatively little waste when compared to adult fish.

Once your fish have grown and are producing more waste (plant food) they will also be able to support the growth of plants with higher nutritional needs, such as tomatoes and squash.

Section 7: Selecting Your Grow Bed and Fish tank

The grow bed and fish tank are the backbone of your aquaponic system and it is therefore crucial that you select these carefully.

Like the ecosystem you are trying to replicate, there needs to be a balance between the amount of waste produced and the number of plants to take up the waste. If there is too much waste in your system, your fish suffer. If there is too little waste, your plants suffer. It is therefore incredibly important to get the ratios right when designing your aquaponic system.

When selecting your grow bed and fish tank, although it may sound obvious, it is absolutely critical that they possess the following qualities: water tightness, strength and non-toxicity. Furthermore, it is important that the material out of which your grow bed and fish tank are made from, are inert, i.e. not able to affect the chemical composition of your aquaponic system.

Grow bed:

When selecting and purchasing your grow bed, it is to be noted that it should be at least 12 inches deep. This will allow you to grow a wide variety of plants (with different root lengths), as well as provide complete and efficient filtration.

Fish tank:

Although space-permitting, I would always suggest that beginners start with a fish tank of greater volume because these are easier to control and the consequences are usually less devastating when an error is made. A 1000+ liters' tank (250 gallons) will generally allow for the most controllable and most sustainable aquaponic garden.

Ultimately however, you can be relatively creative when selecting (and purchasing) the elements that will make up your aquaponic backbone. Among my favorite materials and products to use are stock tanks. I would always opt for stock tanks made of plastic as there are no risks of leached metals or rusting.

If you do opt for the more visual steel stock tanks, make sure you coat or line it to avoid potential leakages of metals. However, you are also free to be a lot more creative. You can recycle old bathtubs, or even explore vertical aquaponic gardening.

For indoor aquaponics, I would highly recommend using an aquarium for the fish tank. Not only are these robust and widely available, but aquariums also make a great home feature, especially when you plan on raising ornamental fish only.

Fish tank to grow bed ratio:

In the beginning stages, I would always recommend that you start with a 1:1 ratio, that is, a grow bed volume which is equal to the volume of your fish tank. Once your system has matured (after approximately 4-6 months), you may wish to add another vegetable grow bed. This 2:1 ratio is often preferred especially when you do plan to keep your fish tank fully stocked at all times.

Now that we have almost covered everything you need to know put together a successful aquaponic system, you are very close to your goal of having your own aquaponic garden unit!

Section 8: Building Your Aquaponic Garden

"True happiness comes from the joy of deeds well done, the zest of creating things new."

- Antoine de Saint-Exupéry (1900 – 1944)

Before we delve into how to build your aquaponic system, I thought this be a good time recap on all the different elements you need to purchase to start assembling your aquaponic garden.

In previous sections, we have discussed the species of plants and species of fish which are well suited to aquaponics. We have also discussed key criteria to keep in mind as well as the different options available when selecting and purchasing a fish tank, grow bed or growing medium.

In this section, before providing you with a step-to-step guide as to how to assemble your system, we will discuss how to choose and select key elements of your plumbing system and how to ensure efficient water circulation.

Aquaponic Shopping List

Substantial parts:

- Fish tank

- Grow bed
- Growing medium
- Dechlorinated water
- Water pump
- Plastic tubing
- Standpipe and timer *OR* bell siphon
- Freshwater test kit

Living components:

- Red worms
- Fish
- Plants

Optional materials:

- Air pump
- Liquid ammonia
- Lights

Choosing the right-sized pump for your aquaponic system

The success of your aquaponic system will depend on the water quality of your system which is ultimately also dependent on high oxygen levels. When it comes to picking the air pump for your fish, a regular aquarium pump will suffice. Because your system is dependent on oxygen, I would highly advise to invest in a reliable air pump.

Arguably, if you replicate the systems as outlined in *section 3*, you will not necessarily need an air pump. This is because the draining action does inject oxygen into your system. I personally however prefer having an air pump just because you can't ever have too much oxygen!

More importantly, effective water circulation is central to the health of your aquaponic system. Your water pump is the heart of your aquaponic garden which circulates the water through the system. Because of this, it is crucial not to cut corners nor skimp when selecting your pump. Mag-drive pumps are best suited to aquaponics. Because the motor is sealed, this eradicates the risk of oil leakage into your water. Whatever choice you make; I would always advise sticking to a trusted source of pump providers.

Plumbing

An ideal and widely-available material for your aquaponic piping is PVC or CPVC. Both materials are inexpensive, food-safe, durable and don't develop rust and are therefore ideally suited to aquaponics.

The grow beds and fish tank need to be connected through plumbing. As explained in *section 3*, there are two ways in which you can achieve the flood and drain effect.

The Timed Flood and Drain System:

1. In this plumbing system, you have a standpipe connecting your grow bed and your fish tank and the water pump is controlled by a timer.
2. The timer, which is attached to the water pump, powers the pump for 15 minutes every 30-45 minutes.
3. During this time, water enters your grow bed 'flooding' your grow bed.
4. After the 15 minutes have expired, the pump switches off.
5. The recycled water in the grow bed then drains through the standpipe back into the fish tank.

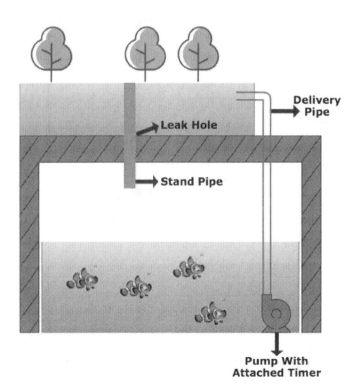

The Auto Siphon System

1. In this system, the pump is continuously pumping water from the fish tank into the grow bed.
2. This pumping causes air to be sucked out of the siphon which triggers a rapid draining of water from the grow bed back down into the fish tank.
3. Once the grow beds are almost entirely drained, air enters the siphon which stops the draining action.
4. At this stage the cycle repeats itself and the grow beds start filling up again.
5. In order to achieve the 'flood and drain', water has to be pumped into the grow beds at a slower rate than the draining action.

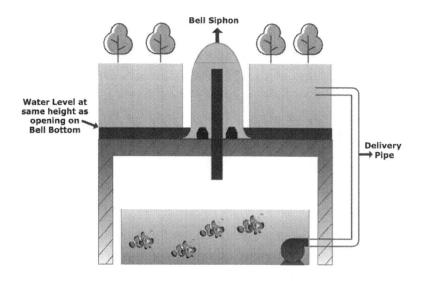

Step-by-Step Guide to Putting Together Your Aquaponic System

1. Wash your growing media and place it into the grow beds.
2. Place the grow bed above the fish tank and connect it to the fish tank via a standpipe or siphon, depending on which of the above plumbing systems you've gone for.
3. Assemble the pump by following the instructions of your specific pump. If your pump contains a filter, feel free to take this out as it is not needed in your aquaponic system, which is self-filtering.
4. Place the pump into your fish tank.
5. Attach piping (called the delivery pipe) to your pump which carries water with fish waste to the grow beds
6. Add dechlorinated water to your fish tank and run the pump.
7. Make sure the water drains back into your fish tank. Speed up or slow down you pump if necessary and regulate the water circulation accordingly.

Once you have assembled your system, you will have to go through a process called 'cycling' before your aquaponic ecosystem is fully established. Cycling is the process of establishing a bacteria colony for your aquaponic system. It is the very thing that will ultimately determine the success of your aquaponic venture.

Section 9: Cycling a New Aquaponics System

"The ecosystem adjusts itself and for every action there is a reaction."

- Steve Mills

Despite our focus on fish and plants, the secret ingredient to the success of your aquaponic system lies with the bacteria and worms that inhabit your grow beds. These are the key actors that transform fish waste into plant fertilizer.

So once your system is set up, the first step is to initiate the nitrogen cycle, a process which is called 'cycling.' I can't stress enough the importance of cycling, which is effectively the creation of an ecosystem. Cycling is also the most daunting and stressful part of setting up an aquaponic system, but the reward is not to be taken lightly. Once your ecosystem is successfully cycled you will be rewarded with a thriving and self-sustaining aquaponic garden.

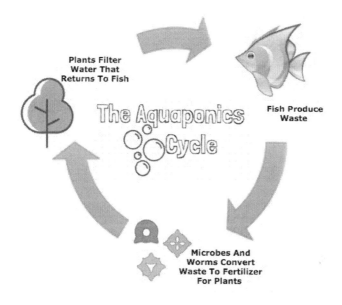

You probably remember this diagram from the beginning of the book and its role here is for you to visualize the nitrogen cycle and its central place in aquaponics. The nitrogen cycle is the process in which the bacteria break down otherwise toxic ammonia and nitrates into nitrites, or, non-toxic food for plants.

The Cycling Process Explained

Cycling begins the moment you or your fish add ammonia to your aquaponic system. It is important to note that ammonia (a compound which contains nitrogen and hydrogen) and nitrites are toxic to fish unless they are broken down or diluted to non-toxic levels.

The presence of ammonia, however, attracts bacteria called Nitrosomonas, which convert ammonia into nitrites. The presence of nitrites in turn attract bacteria called Nitrospira. Nitrospira convert nitrites into nitrates. And nitrates are what we're ultimately after because nitrates = food for plants!

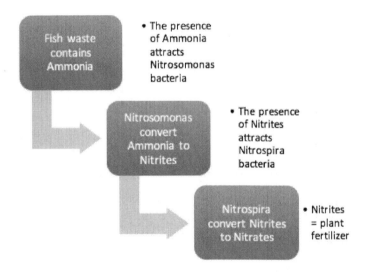

Initiating the cycling process

As explained before, adding ammonia to your fish tank initiates the cycling process. There are two ways to add ammonia: with or without fish.

Roughly 80-90% of the nitrogenous wastes of fish are

excreted as ammonia. Ammonia however, as mentioned earlier, is toxic and can kill your fish if not diluted, removed or converted.

When initiating the cycling process with fish, it is recommended to start with only half as many fish as you would have in a fully stocked tank. Test ammonia and nitrite levels on a daily basis and only feed your fish once a day in order to keep ammonia levels low. Increase fish stock levels only gradually.

Monitoring the cycling process

Cycling with fish is a four- to six-week process during which it is important to monitor your water ensuring that all elements are in range.

For monitoring and testing your water, it is advised to purchase a thermometer as well as a Freshwater Test Kit. The most popular kit, one which I would also highly recommend, is the API Freshwater Master Test Kit, purchasable for a mere $20. This kit is easy to use and specifically designed for aquaponics!

Monitoring and Adjusting pH Level

During cycling, you will need to monitor your tank daily for rising ammonia levels. It is advised to keep the pH levels of your tank at 5.8-7. Higher pH readings suggest higher ammonia levels. pH readings of above 7.0 are therefore problematic as they are indicative of toxic ammonia concentrations.

Adjusting the pH in your aquaponic system

You should at all times maintain a pH level of 6.8-7.0. Again, this is why its best to have a bigger volume of fish tank especially when you're a beginner, because, the more water, the more stable your pH levels.

The best way to stabilize pH levels is to perform a one-third water exchange. In the section below we have included the best methods to raise pH (if it drops below 6.6) and the best methods to lower pH (if it goes above 7.6).

It is also important to note that whenever you introduce water or other elements into your aquaponic system, try and avoid adding anything that contains sodium. Sodium harms your plants and the sodium levels of your water should never rise above 50mg/l.

Raising pH levels

The best way to raise the pH levels of your aquaponic system is to use calcium hydroxide or calcium carbonate. I would highly recommend alternating between the two. On the plus side, these also add calcium and potassium into your aquaponic system which will strengthen your plants.

Lowering pH levels

In order to lower the pH levels, you can use nitric or phosphoric acid. An added benefit of adding these is that your plants also benefit from the nitrate or phosphate that will be released after these acids enter your system.

Nitrite

The other thing you need to monitor during cycling are nitrite levels. Nitrite levels which are too elevated can cause oxygen deprivation, which is equally as devastating for your fish as toxic ammonia concentrations.

Therefore, if your nitrite levels rise to above 10ppm during the cycling process, it is strongly advised to do a water exchange. Exchanging water means diluting the water in your tank by taking roughly a third out and replacing it with clean, dechlorinated water. When performing a water exchange however, make sure that the new water is the same temperature and pH as your tank water.

Besides the water exchange, it is also highly recommended to add some salt to the water. Make sure you only used non-iodized salt and add at least 1 gram of salt per 1 liter of water. Dissolve the salt in a bucket before adding it to the water. Stop feeding your fish until the nitrite levels drop and try to aerate the water as much as possible.

Cycling your system without fish:

An alternative option is to cycle without fish. This method is significantly less stressful as well as quicker. Your system can be fully cycled within 10 – 30 days and at the end of it you can fully stock your tank, which is also an added bonus.

There are many ways in which you can add ammonium to your system. Below are some of them most common methods listed.

- **Urine:** Probably the most natural source, although many people might be opposed to this for various reasons. One thing to keep in mind when using urine is that urine takes a while to convert to ammonia and levels will rise rapidly from one day to another.

- **Liquid ammonia:** When adding liquid ammonia to your system, make sure it is 100% pure ammonia and water. While purchasing ammonia is inexpensive, acquiring pure ammonia can be a difficult task depending on where you live.

- **Ammonium chloride:** This is crystallized ammonia that is readily available in aquarium stores and photography supply stores, among other places.

Once you have selected your source of ammonia, the following is a list of easy-to-follow steps to kick-start your cycling process:

1. Add a little bit of ammonia to your fish tank on a daily basis until you obtain a reading of approximately 2-4 ppm.
2. Make sure you test your ammonia levels daily. If your ammonia levels are nearing 6 ppm, it is advised to stop adding ammonia until its concentration has decreased back to 2-4 ppm.
3. Once nitrites form, reduce the amount of ammonia that you add to your system on a daily basis by 50% until ammonia levels decrease to 2 ppm.
4. Once nitrates appear (5-10 ppm) stop adding ammonia to your fish tank.
5. Add your fish only once ammonia and nitrite levels are both below 0.5 ppm.

Your system is fully cycled once you detect nitrites in your water and once the levels of both nitrates and ammonia have dropped to 0.5 ppm or lower.

Other Things to Consider

Adding plants: It is also recommended to add plants to your aquaponic system as soon as you begin cycling. This will allow them to grow their roots early as well as start removing nitrogen-based waste as soon as possible.

Water temperature: Another thing to keep in mind is that water temperature also has a big effect on the cycling process and particularly the time it takes for your system to become fully cycled. The optimal temperature for cycling is 77 – 86 F°.

Composting worms: Once your aquaponic system is fully cycled and the fish have been added, also add a handful of red wigglers to your grow beds for the best results!

Section 10: Maintaining Your Aquaponic Garden

"Extremes are easy. Strive for balance."

- Colin Wright

Because aquaponics is entirely natural, maintenance is relatively low especially when compared to traditional soil gardening. However, as with any other man-made system, some maintenance is recommended. The checks and tasks recommended below are designed to keep your plants green and fresh and to make sure your fish don't end up like this!

On a Daily Basis:

Feed Your Fish

Feed your fish at least one to two times a day. If your fish aren't eating, this is a sign that they are stressed and an indication that something is wrong. Make sure that the temperature of your water as well as pH level are in the optimal range for your fish (see *Section 5*).

Check Water Temperature

Even if you fish are eating and look happy, it is in the best interest of your fish to also check water temperature on a daily basis. Additionally, check that your pumps are working and that the water is circulating smoothly.

On a Weekly Basis:

Check pH and Ammonia Levels

Once your system is fully cycled, check the pH and ammonia levels of your aquaponic system at least once a week. Obviously, if you receive signs of distressed fish, it is crucial to check pH and ammonia levels immediately and rectify the problem to counter any future disasters.

Check Water Levels and Top Up if Necessary

Furthermore, I also recommend to top up your fish tank once a week, or more often depending on the climate that you find yourself in. When topping up, make sure you use only dechlorinated water with pH levels and a temperature that matches the one of your fish tank.

On a Monthly Basis:

Check Nitrate Levels.

It is likewise advised to check the nitrate levels of your system on a monthly basis. If you can observe a rise in nitrate levels, this is a good indicating that it is time to either plant more plants, add a grow bed or to harvest some of your fish. Try and avoid reaching nitrate levels of more than 150 ppm

Clean Pump and Pipes

Finally, to ensure that the circulatory system of your aquaponic garden is running smoothly, it is advised to clean you pump and pipes once month. This is to avoid any potential clogging inside your pipes.

Section 11: Some Final Considerations: Light, Temperature and Space

"One must maintain a little bit of summer, even in the middle of winter."

- Henry David Thoreau (1817 – 1862)

The plant-fish relationship in aquaponics is one which is found everywhere in nature – in lakes and streams around the earth. Aquaponic cultivation is an ancient hydroculture used around the world. It was used in central Mexico by the Aztec and today is most ordinary in Fast Eastern countries where this technique is used by paddy field farmers.

However, depending where you are situated on earth, you might not share the same hot climate of Mexico or South East Asia. Because of this, it is important to consider a final few things in order to provide the optimal environment for your aquaponic garden.

Climate considerations: growing indoors vs growing outdoors

If you live in a climate where freezing temperatures are the norm in the winter, it is important to consider some alternative options. Unless you have the means and space to erect a greenhouse, the following are the three options open to you:

Harvesting all your crop and fish at the end of summer and shutting down your system over the winter

Not ideal as you would have to go through the cycling process again at the beginning of each summer. The good news is that after a few times, you know the process and what to look out for.

Growing outdoors in the summer and moving your aquaponic system indoors in the winter

Although space-permitting, this option also incurs some practical issues. Portability of your system obviously depends on the size of it. But this option also has many benefits. In the summer, you save energy by using natural heat and light to keep your aquaponic garden in its optimal environment. In the winter, the indoor aquaponic garden will create ambient air by adding humidity and oxygen to your home.

Growing indoors all year round

When growing indoors, beware that aquaponic systems introduce humidity to their environment. Depending where you live, this might be a desired side-effect. When growing indoors, another factor to keep in mind is light. Limited natural light over the winter months may need to be supplemented with additional light sources depending on which plants you grow. While herbs will grow with shorter stints of light, additional light will give you the flexibility to also grow fruiting plants over the winter months.

Below are some indoor lights I would recommend and which are well-suited for indoor aquaponics.

For the hobby grower:

T5 bulbs: These bulbs are inexpensive, energy-efficient and have a broad lighting spectrum. This will allow you to grow both greens as well as fruiting plants indoors. A downside is that these bulbs need replacing every 6 months.

LED lighting: These lights are energy efficient and emit no heat, which is a definite advantage. They are slightly more expensive compared to T5 bulbs. Another added bonus is that these bulbs never need replacing.

For the advanced grower:

HID lighting: HID stands for High Intensity Discharge.

These bulbs are more expensive than the above options but the bulbs last for years and provide a much more intense light.

HID lighting is usually made of four components which you can purchase as separate parts or in a bundle. There are also available optional features.

- **Reflector Hood**, which covers the top of the bulb directing all light down to your plants
- **Remote ballast**, which provides the power to the light
- **Bulb**, which is either a MH (metal halide) or HPS (high-pressure sodium) bulb. MH bulbs are best for vegetative growth, and HPS are best for the flowering stages.
- **Cord set**, which is the power cord which plugs into the ballast and the bulb.
- **Optional**, there are various other optional elements you can add to your lighting system, such as a timer or a fan to blow the heat away from your plants if desired.

Section 12: Last but Not Least

"There are no gardening mistakes, only experiments."

- *Janet Kilburn Phillips*

I would like to take this opportunity to thank you for reading this book. I hope you now have a solid foundation on the process, and that you're equipped with the knowledge to put you on the path to becoming an aquaponic success!

My final piece of advice - no matter how diligent you are in your research, your best learning will come from doing, so don't hesitate in getting started. Start simple, perhaps with one of the basic systems outlined and with a easier crop such as lettuce and herbs. Once you put your knowledge into practice you'll soon have the skills to advance onto more challenging systems and growing vine and fruit plants. I recommend revisiting the sections along with careful further research to constantly refresh your knowledge as you progress.

I sincerely wish you the best of luck in your aquaponic adventure.

Best wishes,

Andy Jacobson

39634149R00077

Made in the USA
Middletown, DE
18 March 2019